Bride's

Little Headaches

before the big day!

ROCK POINT

A division of the Quarto Publishing Group USA Inc.
276 Fifth Avenue Suite 206
New York, New York 10001

ROCK POINT and the distinctive Rock Point logo are trademarks of
the Quarto Publishing Group USA Inc

This 2014 edition published by Rock Point
by arrangement with Harriet Ziefert, Inc.

ISBN-13: 978-1-631060-10-6

Printed in China

2 4 6 8 10 9 7 5 3 1

just engaged

just engaged
little headaches

*F*eeling certain
you *can* get it all done—
if you don't eat, sleep, or work.
No problem!

just engaged
little headaches

*D*reaming
about the "To-Do" list.
Waking up with it
stuck to your face.

just engaged
little headaches

$\mathcal{C}$hoosing a date
that doesn't conflict with anyone's
birthday,
anniversary,
vacation,
memorial service,
bar mitzvah,
or
your best friend's wedding.

just engaged
little headaches

*F*eeling stuck between your fiancé's
"whatever you want is fine with me"
and your future mother-in-law's
"well, in my day…"

just engaged
little headaches

blah
blah
blah

$\mathcal{G}$etting wedding advice
from your mother,
your grandmother,
your future mother-in-law,
your married friends,
your unmarried friends,
the lady on the bus who saw you
reading *Brides* magazine,
your gynecologist,
your pet groomer,
the guy who made your
morning coffee….

just engaged
little headaches

*E*ndlessly repeating,
"We're just having a few friends
and the immediate family,"
as the guest list reaches 200-and-counting.

just engaged
little headaches

*L*imiting the guest list to
just close friends
and family,
and certain colleagues,
and former classmates,
and
people you see all the time who will feel hurt,
and
people who will give great gifts
and might not even come,
and…

just engaged
little headaches

*T*rying to find
a Jewish-Catholic-Atheist-Hindu
officiant.

just engaged
little headaches

$\mathcal{C}$hoosing a venue that's
romantic,
the right size,
elegant,
rustic,
casual,
formal,
natural,
lavish,
comfortable,
dazzling,

and affordable!

just engaged
little headaches

$\mathcal{B}$eing unable to stop
staring at your hand.

$\mathcal{E}$veryone asking to see the ring.

$\mathcal{W}$orrying about losing it.

$\mathcal{T}$hinking,
"No matter what,
I'm keeping the ring!"

just engaged
little headaches

$\mathcal{F}$antasizing about doing a "quickie"
in Vegas or even...
how much fun it might be
to ELOPE!

LITTLE HEADACHES

The Dress

the dress
little headaches

The neckline:
Sweetheart?
Plunging?
Halter?
High-necked?
One-shouldered?
Strapless?
Totally
boob-a-licious?

*T*he dress:
white, ivory, cream, ecru, or—
hey, pink?

New, old, borrowed, or—

*S*leeves? Belt?
Beads? Lace?
A-line? Princess? Trumpet?
Bustle? Corset?
What the heck is tea length?

*W*ill an
Empire silhouette
make me look
pregnant?

the dress
little headaches

*W*ill this much lace
make me look like
a tablecloth?

*W*ill I be able to breathe?

*W*ill this much bling
make me look trashy?

the dress
little headaches

*H*mmm...
will Grandma faint
if I wear a dress that
shows all the
tattoos?

the dress
little headaches

If the dress is long enough—
can I wear sneakers?

If the heels are four inches,
will I be taller
than my groom?

Should I wear cowboy boots,
Cinderella slippers, or
gladiator sandals?

the dress
little headaches

$\mathcal{C}$hoosing the dress you really want,
or making a down payment
on a condo?

$\mathcal{I}$ love this dress!
It's <u>HOW</u> much?

the dress
little headaches

*N*umber 37 is IT!
If they can change
the skirt
and the neckline,
get rid of the bustle,
add some beading,
and…

NEXT!

the dress
little headaches

$\mathscr{B}$acon cheeseburger—
or the custom-made,
size-six gown you
just ordered.

the dress
little headaches

Pro:

You're down two sizes!

Con:

Your engagement ring keeps falling off.
Splash!
Into the sink.
Down the toilet.
Gone!

the dress
little headaches

*D*iscovering that your head
and a tiara
are not made for each other.
You look more like the Burger King
and less like Princess Kate.

*K*nowing that even in something
white, lacy, and utterly traditional,
you'll never pull off
"virgin."

*T*he dress of your dreams
makes you look like
a doughboy.

*I*t looked so perfect
in the catalogue
on the totally airbrushed,
six-foot-tall, size-zero model!

the dress
little headaches

*F*inding a bridesmaid dress
that will look fabulous on someone
short,
tall,
dark,
fair,
curvy,
skinny,
busty,
flat-chested,
and/or pregnant . . .

and doesn't clash with
the flowers and tablecloths.

the dress
little headaches

*H*e saw you in the dress.

Is risking bad luck worth
giving up the $1,000 deposit?

*C*onvincing your fiancé that it is.

The Cake

the cake
little headaches

*H*uge, expensive,
seven-tiered masterpiece?
Hmmm.
Cupcakes—why not?
Cake pops? Possibly.

An individual minature
wedding cake for each guest?

the cake
little headaches

Chocolate torte?
Carrot cake?
Amaretto and blueberry?
Lemon drizzle sponge?
Spiced toffee apple?
Madagascar vanilla sponge?
Raspberry and white chocolate?
Exotic coconut?
Strawberry champagne?
Hazelnut almond?
Fondant?
Buttercream?
Ganache?

Donuts, please!

the cake
little headaches

*D*isagreeing about
the kind of cake with your
fiancé,
mother,
sister,
cousin,
aunt,
best friend,
hairdresser,
dentist's assistant,
the woman behind you on line
at the post office.

*Y*ou are totally on the same page—
chocolate-coconut-raspberry filling.
Mmmm.

Still, best to have one more round
of tasting "just to be sure."
Mmmm-mmm.

Maybe just one more.

the cake
little headaches

*"Honey, I love you.
But we are not having a cake
made out of
brownies."*

the cake
little headaches

*D*iscovering
that the cake wizard *can* create
a replica of the yacht
he proposed on.
But it won't fit through the door.

the cake
little headaches

*F*inding a vegan baker
because your fiancé's
sister is vegetarian.

*C*an you make buttercream
with artificial sweetner?

*G*luten free?
Yum!

the cake
little headaches

Realizing
you can have your dream cake if:
You get your dress at Target.
You cut down the guest list to ten.
You cancel the honeymoon.
You have the dinner delivered by
a Chinese take-out place.

Or take out another loan.

the cake
little headaches

*B*aking your own cake for 200—
too ambitious.

*T*elling your aunt that
her famous fruitcake
will not fit with your theme.

the cake
little headaches

*Y*our first,
second, and third choice of bakers
are booked for the next two years,
except on Halloween.

*Y*our first,
second, and third choice of venues
are booked except on the date
of your best friend's wedding.

the cake
little headaches

*I*t's dazzling,
original,
a feast for the eyes.
And it tastes
like cardboard
and kindergarten paste.

the cake
little headaches

*L*osing your ability
to feel your tongue
after fifteen tastings
at five different caterers.

Cake mix
is starting to seem
very appealing.

the cake
little headaches

*A*fter tasing six different cakes
in under an hour…

Pro:
With all the sugar pumping
through your system,
you are a superwoman!
Capable of anything!

Con:
But first you need to throw up.

the cake
little headaches

*F*eeling a strange compulsion
to bite off the little heads of the
bride and groom on your
wedding-cake topper.

Planning
The Event

*T*he invitations
correctly list the date as the 19th of May.
But you are Joanna,
not Johann!

*T*he graceful cursive font
that you've chosen
has a capital 'T' that looks like
a capital 'F,'
and your last name is Tucker.

planning the event
little headaches

*F*inding out that
the Most Beautiful Place,
which you've dreamed
of for your wedding
is now…
Golden Pins Bowling Alley.

planning the event
little headaches

*T*he one thing your fiancé insists on
is the color scheme—
the colors of his favorite football team:
steel-gray and maroon.

planning the event
little headaches

*M*oving Aunt Teresa,
who just divorced Uncle Jack,
over to Table 8 means
you'll have to move Aunt Jane,
who is not speaking to Aunt Teresa, to Table 9,
which will put Aunt Jane at the same table
with Travis, the Make-out King,
who will put the moves on Aunt Jane,
who loves to drink at weddings,
and flirt, and…

planning the event
little headaches

First dance song—first argument!
City Bride wants
"The Way You Look Tonight."
Country Groom is hot for
"Shotgun Wedding."

planning the event
little headaches

*F*inding a band
that can play something
more modern than
Motown.

*T*elling your fiancé's brother
that you'll take a pass on his band called
Devil Ate My Dingo.

planning the event
little headaches

Chicken

Chicken Marsala

Glazed Chicken with Mushrooms

Tomato Basil Chicken

Chicken Cordon Bleu

Chicken Kiev

Apple Nut Stuffed Chicken Breast

Apricot Chicken

Lemon Herb Chicken

Chicken Tuscany

and then there's . . .

planning the event
little headaches

Beef

Roast Beef Wellington

Marinated Beef Tips

Prime Rib

Filet Mignon

or perhaps . . .

Fish

Garlic Roasted Cod

Cajun Catfish Filets

Herb Crusted Salmon . . .

Can we just give everyone a bowl of mac'n'cheese
and be done with it?

$\mathcal{T}$ulips? Day lilies?
Out of season!

But there are mums and
carnations aplenty!

You've always wanted
your wedding to look like
a ninth-grade prom!

planning the event
little headaches

*W*aking up in a cold sweat
about what the Best Man,
Maid of Honor,
and various drunk relatives
might decide to say.

*E*xplaining to your wedding planner
that your budget cannot accommodate
a flock of doves,
a golden horse-drawn carriage,
5,000 individually crafted origami swans,
a live performance by Mariah Carey,
and a custom-made suit for the groom
to match the color scheme.

planning the event
little headaches

$\mathcal{S}$electing a ceremony reading
that won't offend
the True Believers,
the Cynics,
the Attention-Impaired,
and the Swoony Romantics.

planning the event
little headaches

*T*rying to accommodate guests
who are on diets,
vegan,
food snobs,
allergic,
lactose intolerant,
kosher,
and are afraid of anything
"ethnic."

planning the event
little headaches

*B*eing in
total agreement about:

open bar!

*B*eing in
total disagreement about:

EVERYTHING
ELSE!

LITTLE HEADACHES

The Honeymoon

the honeymoon
little headaches

Pro:

Relaxing tropical resort

Con:

Unpredictable monsoons

Pro:

Action-packed, mountain-climbing adventure

Con:

Sprains, falls, avalanches

the honeymoon
little headaches

Pro:
Camping under the stars

Con:
Inquisitive, hungry bears,
uninvited raccoons, snakes, bugs

Pro:
Snorkeling in Hawaii

Con:
Stingrays, sharks, lobster-red sunburns

the honeymoon
little headaches

Pro:
Disney World-a-Rama

Con:
Lines of crabby kids making you rethink
the whole parent thing

Pro:
The exotic allure of Bali

Con:
The non-exotic 100% humidity

the honeymoon
little headaches

Pro:
The romance of Paris

Con:
The contempt of the French

Pro:
Golfing in Scotland

Con:
Being served pancreas for dinner

the honeymoon
little headaches

Pro:

Any place fashionable and fabulous!

Con:

The price tag!

the honeymoon
little headaches

Pro:

Getting away to start your life together

Con:

NONE!

LITTLE HEADACHES

The
Final Push...

Off The Cliff?

the final push
little headaches

*Y*our To-Do list
has finally shrunk…
by 10 percent.

*G*etting pre-wedding
carpal tunnel syndrome…
from writing checks.

the final push
little headaches

$\mathcal{D}$iscovering that
your amateur calligraphy has
caused many guests
to think the reception
will be in Newark,
instead of New York.

the final push
little headaches

*H*aving your hair and makeup preview.
Accepting that no matter what,
you'll never look like Cameron Diaz.

*A*fter increasing your workout
to three times a week, your
arms still refuse to become
Michelle Obama-like.

the final push
little headaches

*I*gnoring your Visa bill.
And the one from American Express...
and MasterCard
and...
forget about your savings account!

The Day

the day
little headaches

*F*eeling excited,
overwhelmed,
cherished, loved,
nervous, thrilled…
and totally nauseous.

I'm the bride.
I'm not allowed to have a zit.

the day
little headaches

*Y*ou ordered sunshine
and a blue sky!
Not rain.
Not humidity.
Not clouds.

the day
little headaches

*F*inding out that
the butterflies
in your stomach
can't handle champagne.

*T*rying to be sympathetic
when your flower girl throws a tantrum
and screams,
"I wanna go to Chuck E. Cheese!"

the day
little headaches

*M*aking sure that your bum,
but not the dress,
makes it onto the toilet.

*S*o glad you chose to have the train.
So dramatic.
So beautiful.
So statement-making.
So...*ripped!*

the day
little headaches

*C*ringing through
the World's Most Embarrassing Toast
from the World's Drunkest Best Man.

*S*miling as way too many details
about the bachelorette party
are revealed during your
"Maid of Dishonor's" toast.

the day
little headaches

The Thong Song?
Who told the DJ he could play

The Thong Song?
And there's Grandma
getting her groove on!

Confirming what you suspected all along:
Aunt Enid should never twerk.

the day
little headaches

*Y*ou're finally in your honeymoon suite.
As soon as you remove 500 bobby pins
out of your shellacked hair,
and undo the zillion tiny buttons
on the back of your dress,
well then,
it'll be time for…breakfast!

the day
little headaches

*Y*ou did.

*H*e did.

*Y*ou are!

YIPPEE!

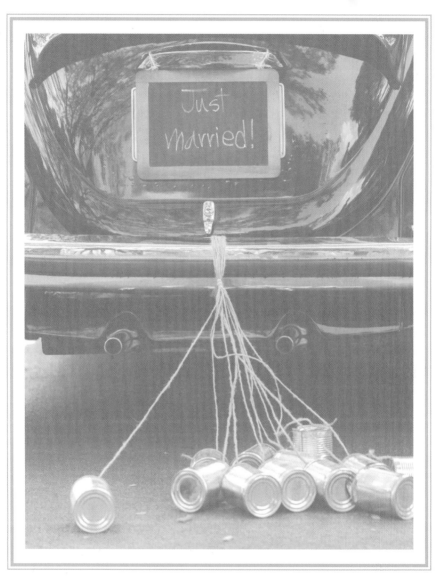